# NO COMPROMISE

*An Urban Guide to Urban Youth Ministry*

DEDICATED TO PATRICK D. HAMPTON

# BOBBY HAMPTON JR.

Copyright © 2016 by Bobby Hampton
All rights reserved. This book or any portion thereof may not be reproduced or used in any manner whatsoever without the express written permission of the publisher except for the use of brief quotations in a book review.

**Limits of Liability and Disclaimer of Warranty**

The author and publisher shall not be liable for your misuse of this material. This book is strictly for informational and educational purposes. The purpose of this book is to educate and entertain. The author and/or publisher do not guarantee that anyone following these techniques, suggestions, tips, ideas, or strategies will become successful. The author and/or publisher shall have neither liability nor responsibility to anyone with respect to any loss or damage caused, or alleged to be caused, directly or indirectly by the information contained in this book.

Views expressed in this publication do not necessarily reflect the views of the publisher.

Printed in the United States of America

ISBN 978-0-9982523-4-6

Keen Vision Publishing

www.keen-vision.com

*For youth leaders worldwide…*

# ACKNOWLEDGEMENTS

Over the course of my life, God has allowed me to meet, partner, and connect with some amazing individuals. I am so grateful for your impact and influence in my life.

To my wife, Tiffany Hampton. Thank you so much for your unconditional love and support. I am honored that God deemed me worthy to cover, lead, and protect you for life. To my amazing children, Dorian and Bailey, Daddy loves you! To my awesome parents, Bobby and Patricia Hampton, thank you for every sacrifice you made for me. I pray I've made you two proud!

To my pastor, Dr. E. Dewey Smith, thank you for living a lifestyle of true leadership. I am grateful for the opportunity to serve. To The House of Hope Atlanta, Wendell Martin, Pastor Thomas L. Murray, Anointed Temple of Praise Church, Pastor T.C. Johnson, & St. Luke Christian Church, I am so thankful for the positive impact you all have made on my life.

Last, but not least, to you, the reader. Thank you for reading this book. Your support means the world to me. I pray this book blesses you, your youth ministry, and your church.

Bobby Hampton Jr.

# ABOUT THE AUTHOR

Minister Bobby Hampton Jr. is the fourth and youngest son of Bobby and Patricia Hampton. He was born in Chattanooga, Tennessee. During his early years, the Lord called his father to pastor Hawkinsville Missionary Baptist Church. There, he learned to value the culture and benefits of a Christian life. At the early age of eight he received, confessed, and accepted Jesus as his personal Savior. Little did he know, this would be the start of a new beginning of his Christian journey! After receiving Christ, he was actively involved in church youth ministry and joined youth groups in his community.

After graduating from Tyner High School, God allowed him to receive an athletic scholarship to Alabama A&M University. While attending college, Min. Hampton began to see everything the world had to offer and its ability to make or break a person through decisions made. Through prayer and fasting, God did not allow the college lifestyle to dictate his future. He remained focused and began a youth ministry in the city of Huntsville, Alabama with a mission of seeing young people saved! On the fourth Sunday in July 2003, he accepted the call to ministry. On December 14, 2003 he preached his initial sermon at Hawkinsville Missionary Baptist Church under the leadership of his father.

Min. Hampton started The No Compromise Youth Movement in Memphis, TN bringing thousands of young people to Christ! This movement partnered with Memphis City School and the City of Memphis to help fight off local gangs. Now, The No Compromise Youth Movement has developed into a nationally known youth movement for young people across the nation.

In addition to youth ministry, Min. Hampton was formerly employed by the Rockdale County School System, and is pursuing his graduate studies at Union University concentrating on his Master of Divinity Degree. Min. Hampton serves as youth pastor at Greater Travelers Rest Baptist Church under Pastor E. Dewey Smith Jr. He knew that this would be the best place to learn more about God and in return, relate the knowledge obtained to a generation that has the ability to change the world through leadership in the church and community involvement.

# CONTENTS

ACKNOWLEDGEMENTS ........................................... v

FOREWORD ........................................................ 1

## PART ONE: KNOW THE VISION

**Chapter One**

PASTOR & YOUTH PASTOR RELATIONSHIP ................... 5

**Chapter Two**

THE CULTURE OF THE CHURCH ................................. 11

## PART TWO: BUILD THE TEAM

**Chapter Three**

BUILDING YOUR TEAM ............................................. 17

**Chapter Four**

SLOW GROWTH VS FAST GROWTH ........................... 23

## PART THREE: THE MINISTRY & YOU

**Chapter Five**

BIBLE BASED PRINCIPLES ......................................... 31

## Chapter Six

THE YOUTH PASTOR WITHIN ......................................35

What's Next? ........................................................41

STAY CONNECTED ...............................................43

# FOREWORD

The Urban Guide to Youth Ministry is a holistic leadership guide to equip you with the inspiration, information, skills and qualities you need to lead an outstanding youth ministry.

Bobby Hampton Jr. packed this book with practical insights that breaks down the broad subject of youth ministry into comprehensible components and simplistic formats that inspire, motivate and transform. Your talents will be awakened, your potential stirred and your skills honed so you can be the best youth leader you can be. The leadership principles and qualities taught cut across every walk of life.

Author Bobby L. Hampton Jr. is a successful youth leadership consultant who has led several youth ministries to greatness. He knows what it takes to build outstanding leaders and volunteers. He leads one of the fastest growing youth ministries in the nation, and he has poured out his heart on the subject in The Urban Guide for Youth Ministry. It will not only to transform your thinking but to lead you on the journey to becoming a leader in your home, your workplace, your church, your community and even your nation.

Patrick D. Hampton
National Youth Strategist and Youth Activist

# PART ONE
# KNOW THE VISION

# Chapter One
## PASTOR & YOUTH PASTOR RELATIONSHIP

One of the leading causes of failing youth ministries is the neglected relationship between a Senior Pastor and the Youth Pastor. If there is no clear vision from the senior pastor as it relates to the youth ministry, youth ministries are bound to fail! I've had the opportunity to work under many pastors, community leaders, and youth pastors. Some leaders had clear visions while others lacked knowledge of youth ministry and were therefore unable to clearly communicate how they wanted their youth ministry to look. In this chapter, you will learn steps to better enhance your relationship with your senior pastor and tips on how to navigate through difficult issues.

### KNOW YOUR PASTOR'S VISION

Remember, this is not your ship! God has given your senior pastor the assignment to shepherd His sheep. It is vital that you immerse yourself in the church's culture (which we'll discuss more in the next chapter) and observe your senior pastor's pattern, decision making, and vision casting. When your senior pastor is casting vision, it's important that you take note of key elements and be creative in implementing them in your youth ministry. This tells your senior pastor that you are on the same page and ready to follow. Some youth pastors I've known through the years have come into a church with their own agenda and don't last one minute. Why? They didn't take the time to know the senior pastor and flow with the vision God gave him. My current position as youth pastor at the House of Hope Atlanta under the leadership of Dr. E. Dewey Smith Jr. is a perfect example of how to build a great relationship between a senior pastor and a youth pastor. When I was selected as youth pastor, we had a very important conversation right at the beginning. Pastor Smith clearly explained the vision of the church. I knew what the measure of my success would be based upon. Pastor Smith's vision was very reachable and tangible, even though he is the pastor of a mega-church that has over 10,000 members. He knew how important youth ministry was to the ministry God gave him. He was clear about what he wanted and what the ministry needed. That made it much easier to follow the previous youth pastor who established a great foundation upon which to build. Any youth ministry with a strong foundation is guaranteed to succeed!

## SUPPORT YOUR PASTOR

Loyalty goes a long way! It's very important that you remain supportive and loyal to your senior pastor. There are three ways to support your senior pastor: Time, Talent, and Treasures.

**TIME** After speaking with a few senior pastors about this, time was the one subject that kept ringing out. Time is very valuable. Don't waste their time! The saddest thing a youth pastor/leader can do is make excuses about why he/she wasn't given the time or the opportunity to do their assignment. People who make excuses about their assignments are those who didn't study or prepare for them. Again, don't waste your senior pastor's time. Better yet, don't waste God's time. If God has called you to youth ministry be called to youth ministry until God and the senior pastor releases you to another ministry focus. Spend time in the Word. Spend time with the youth you minister to. As a youth leader, you must spend time engaging this generation.

Youth ministry goes beyond the four walls of the church. Develop a time management plan that will allow you to focus on making an effective youth ministry. The worst thing a senior pastor can have on their staff is someone who is slothful and mismanages their time! Cherish your moments in youth ministry by developing time management skills.

**TALENT** Many youth pastors are multi-talented. For example, I'm a youth pastor by calling, but I'm also a graphic designer, musician, and a certified professional teacher. I make sure that the youth ministry benefits from all of these gifts. I'm able to write a song for the youth choir and promote the ministry on social media by creating graphics for the youth ministry. I put to use every gift God has placed in me. Your talents are valuable to the youth ministry. Never limit yourself! Youth ministry can also be a time of preparation for your next season. Don't give God half of you. Give Him all of you!

**TREASURE** Make sure you are giving God your treasures. Treasures are those things you sacrifice for the sake of the ministry. Tithing is a very important principal to practice. Tithing allows you and the ministry you lead to be blessed. In The Message Bible, it states in Malachi 3:10-11, "Bring your full tithe to the Temple treasury so there will be ample provisions in my Temple. Test me in this and see if I don't open up heaven itself to you and pour out blessings beyond your wildest dreams. For my part, I will defend you against marauders, protect your wheat fields and vegetable gardens against plunderers." Notice the first clause: bring your tithe to the Temple so there will be provision in the Temple. You want a bigger budget? TITHE! Watch God make provision for the ministry. Let's take a look at the "B" clause of the text. God makes a bold statement and suggests that you try Him and watch Him bless you for your sacrifice to the ministry.

## NAVIGATE THROUGH UNCLEAR VISION

For many youth pastors across the country, navigating through unclear vision can be challenging. What do you do if your senior pastor has no clue about youth ministry and hasn't given you any measures of success? This can be difficult and frustrating. It's important that you look at the overall vision of the church. Sometimes, your pastor has an overall vision and is more focused on it rather than your specific vision for the youth ministry. If this is the case, please mimic the overall vision. Again, this allows your pastor to see that you are willing to follow.

If you have a new idea or concept, please don't implement any concept or idea without the approval of your senior pastor. Allow your pastor to be the first to hear about the idea and give his input. This will help you gauge the direction he is going in with the overall vision. For example, if your pastor dislikes Christian rap and he thinks it doesn't make sense, it is not a good idea to plan a holy hip-hop concert. On the other hand, you might have an "Out of the Box" pastor who loves Christian rap. This would make your church an ideal environment for a concert.

It's vital and important that we use these suggestions to help make our senior pastor comfortable and at ease about who's over the youth ministry. Again, remember, it's not your ship! By implementing these concepts, you will find that your relationship with your senior pastor is stronger and you will have an enjoyable experience in youth ministry.

# Chapter Two
## THE CULTURE OF THE CHURCH

When understanding the culture of a particular ministry, you must first know where it started. The culture of a church can tell you the who's, what's, when's, where's and why's of the ministry. It's important that you spend time learning your church culture. It will better help you navigate through and avoid potential problems. The culture of the church is defined as the atmosphere in which the church functions. I know you are asking what this has to do with youth ministry. Trust me, it has a lot to do with youth ministry. Your youth ministry will be a direct reflection of the church's culture. If you have a healthy church culture, you will have a healthy youth ministry. If the culture is unhealthy, you will possibly have an unhealthy youth ministry. Breaking unhealthy cultures can be difficult. It can be a daunting task to combat anything that is standing. Hopefully, you will know how do this effectively after you read this chapter on church culture.

## BREAKING UNHEALTHY CULTURES

In order to break unhealthy cultures in youth ministry, such as low involvement and entitled parents and kids, you must first examine the youth ministry as a whole. What's working and what isn't working? Allow your parents and youth to redefine the youth ministry. Allow them to even implement their ideas as they redefine church! They will begin to create their own healthy positive climates. Your participation numbers will increase and the youth won't be entitled, but will be owners of their ministry.

Youth ministries across the nation have suffered due to lack of church involvement. In some cases, the youth ministry is considered to be a babysitting service rather than a student ministry. If you feel like your youth ministry is a babysitting service, it's time to change the culture! This sounds difficult, but don't worry; what follows are some great ways to change culture and the environment.

## STEP 1: SURVEY PARENTS

This step will allow you access to how the parent feels about the state of the youth ministry. Use probing questions. Here's an example.

*What would you like the youth ministry to focus on this year?*
   A. Fellowship (events, fun and games)
   B. Evangelism (Service projects)
   C. Discipleship (Bible Study, worship service, Sunday school)
   D. Worship & Arts (Step team, Mime and choir)

Questions like this will give you a lot of information. If the parent selects "A", of course you know they want the youth ministry to stay as a baby-sitting service. If their answer is "B", this would indicate a great opportunity to develop an Outreach Ministry. Your youth ministry will be known for doing things for the community. If their answer is "C", this will let you know to enhance those particular aspects of your youth ministry. If their answer is "D", start putting in ministries that the youth will be actively involved in.

## STEP 2: REVIEW WITH SENIOR PASTOR

Go over the surveys with your senior pastor. Before you storm into his or her office, however, please do your research on other youth ministries that have been successful in the different areas of ministry that the surveys indicate you should discuss.

## STEP 3: FOCUS ON YOUR STRENGTHS

If your strengths are outreach and the youth like helping the homeless, community clean ups, and mission trips, then that's your strength! Many times as youth leaders, we spend so much time focusing on ideas that will never fit in the church culture. You will stress yourself out trying to make something fit that doesn't belong. We will talk about that more in upcoming chapters! Below are a few more tips to maintain a healthy culture in the youth ministry.

Contrary to what you're probably thinking, even having a healthy culture in youth ministry can be very dangerous. You can become comfortable in what you are doing and fail to evolve. A healthy youth ministry consistently changes. It's always moving, and never gets stuck! What can you do to maintain a healthy culture in your youth ministry? Never get comfortable in a healthy state. Unhealthy moments will always appear! Stay in tune with the NOW generation. Always flow with the Senior Pastor. Finally, be in line with God!

# Part Two
## Build the Team

# Chapter Three
## BUILDING YOUR TEAM

In most urban youth ministries, volunteers are very important. Most of us wish we had a paid staff to handle the day-to-day operations of the youth ministry. Unfortunately, urban youth ministries thrive off of unpaid volunteers. This can be both a good thing and a bad thing. In fact, here are five types of youth ministry volunteers:

1. Passionate Volunteers
2. Committed Volunteers
3. Needy Volunteers
4. Opportunistic Volunteers
5. Event-Driven Volunteers

**Passionate volunteers** are individuals who are passionate about youth ministry. God has called them to be actively involved within the ministry. Passionate volunteers are there no matter what. They are equipped with gifts that will help you sustain a youth ministry. These types of volunteers work well with leading events, small groups, Bible studies and mentoring the youth. Although they are very strong, they too have weaknesses. Be very careful with how you address passionate volunteers. They can be very headstrong about what they're passionate about. Allow them to flourish and never put them in a box. If you have two volunteers that fit in this category, you are doing well!

**Committed volunteers** are individuals who are committed to the youth ministry, but lack passion. This type of volunteer will be there for the youth ministry only for the cause. Be careful. It is easy to confuse committed volunteers with passionate volunteers. They look and work like passionate volunteers, but are only there to fulfill their commitment. When the commitment is fulfilled, in most cases they will find a new commitment to attach themselves to.

**Needy volunteers** are individuals who are trying to fulfill a need for themselves. As soon as the need is fulfilled, they will abandon their assignment with the youth ministry. This type of volunteer will drain you as a leader because they are looking for the thing they need rather than fulfilling the need of the child. They join the youth ministry out of guilt, therefore serve out of guilt rather than serving the youth.

**Opportunistic volunteers** are individuals who seek to establish an opportunity to enhance their own personal ministry. They come to the youth with an agenda and will always try to devalue your decision, establish cliques, and duplicate themselves within the group. If you do not have structure in place, they will have a field day sowing bad seeds on fertile ground. They are only there for opportunity.

**Event-driven volunteers** are individuals who only show up for major events. They are the first ones to purchase t-shirts, but never attend planning meetings. Event-driven volunteers are all about the lights, camera, and action. You will need these volunteers for your big events.

## IDENTIFYING STRENGTHS & WEAKNESSES

Think about the volunteers in your youth ministry and identify what category they would fit into. Be sure to prayerfully select volunteers that best suit your ministry. This may take some time, but eventually the right people will arrive. Placing volunteers in the wrong category can be detrimental to the ministry. Once you have identified which category your volunteers fit into, you will be able to quickly identify their strengths and weaknesses.

Each volunteer will have a strength and weakness. It is important that you have a process in place for each potential volunteer to go through before they are placed in your youth ministries.

**Pre- Interview Stage** This stage is when the potential volunteers have agreed to be a part of the youth ministry. They will answer questions about their personal lives, experiences in youth ministry, and strengths and weaknesses.

**Background Check** This stage of the process is when potential volunteers submit an application and a background check is performed. The background check helps identify predators, sex offenders and fraudulent activity. The application process lasts seven days. This gives me time to evaluate the volunteer and go into deep prayer about who will be mentoring the youth.

**Observation Period** This period is very important to the process. The observation period allows the potential volunteer to see the youth ministry in its entirety. The volunteers will observe the youth ministry for 30 days and at the end of the observation period, each volunteer will determine where he or she best fits the youth ministry.

**Post-Interview** This stage is for the individual to meet with student leaders of the youth ministry and youth pastor. In this interview, students will ask questions about everything from relating to teens, to teaching a Bible study.

When building a healthy team, establishing a good relationship with your volunteers is important. This will help you see their strengths and weaknesses and compartmentalize your volunteers into the categories listed above, therefore limiting burn out among volunteers.

# Chapter Four
## SLOW GROWTH VS FAST GROWTH

When it comes to understanding how to grow your youth ministry, there are two ways of thinking that can help you. I call them the "Brewing Your Tea" concept and the "Just Add Water" concept. I believe these two concepts will help you in any situation you walk into.

**BREWING YOUR TEA**

In order to understand this method, you must understand how you brew tea. Here are the steps:

**Step One: Watch the water!**
Water is the base for tea. Water must be filtered and go through a process before being merged with other ingredients. Bad filtrations can cause sickness and even death if the water is not processed right. In youth ministry, if you do have the right base

(foundation), it can possible destroy the entire youth ministry in the long run.

## Step Two: Choose the right brand!

When brewing tea, choosing the right brand is important! The brand determines the quality of the batch. Consumers know that they can keep coming back to get the same product and get the same quality result. In youth ministry, if you are not careful, you might try to go the cheap route and lose quality in your youth ministry because of a bad brand choice.

## Step Three: Add the unexpected!

When adding flavor to your tea, the first ingredient you pick up is sugar. Although sugar is great for your taste buds, it's also harmful to your health. It's important that we add substance to the tea, and preferably substances that don't bring a negative side effect that can harm the body. Many youth ministries have tried to add a lot of stuff, but it turns out to have a negative side effect. Add something to your youth ministry that will stick and stay. A stable youth ministry is like heaven to a parent.

## JUST ADD WATER

The second concept is what I call "Just Add Water." Have you ever made a batch of Kool-Aid? Everything is premixed and ready to for someone to open the package and just add water. Water is added to unlock the flavor that is within the package. This concept is designed for youth pastor/youth leaders that will be stepping into a particular ministry that has a strong foundation, functional programs and a developed volunteer core. Most of the time, you will find this type of youth ministry in progressive churches with a strong focus on youth ministries.

When walking into this type of youth ministry, you would need to spend time observing. This can be a fast-paced environment! If you are not careful, you will lose yourself in the process. Don't try to do too much, when much has already been done. JUST ADD WATER!! Find the ingredient that will allow the youth ministry to flourish!

Fast growth can be fun and detrimental at the same time. I remember when I was youth pastor at a smaller church. I had so many ideas and was ready to work. I implemented a mentorship program, connected with the community and developed youth leaders. I did all of this in one year's time. Everything that the pastor wanted done in the first year, I accomplished in the first 3 months. Youth began to flood the ministry but its infrastructure was not developed. Communication was horrible, parents were upset and most importantly it resulted in a burned out youth pastor. Why? I was looking at the numbers rather than the structure.

Never base the success of your youth ministry on strictly numbers. Numbers can fool you into thinking you have a thriving youth ministry but you really have a shallow ankle! If not treated properly, it can cause long-term complications. If you find yourself in this position, quickly assemble a team that can handle these 3 areas:

1. Communication
2. Logistics
3. Follow-up

Slow growth is different! Slow growth allows you to develop a stable ministry and programs that can sustain your ministry for many years. The volunteers will not be burned out and the kids will enjoy being a part of a ministry that is focused. Your parents will be pleased with the communication and well-thought-out events. Ask yourself these questions:

1. What concept better fits your ministry?

2. What steps should you take to enhance the growth of your youth ministry?
3. What plan do you have in place to handle fast growth?

# Part Three
## THE MINISTRY & YOU

# Chapter Five
## BIBLE BASED PRINCIPLES

I truly believe that we are not giving the Bible a fair shot in our churches and in our youth ministries. Somewhere along the way, we started focusing on fun and games rather than the Bible and spiritual disciplines. Youth pastors and leaders have taken away true biblical teaching and substituted it for watered-down inspirational speaking. The question is, are these plans and programs bringing kids to the "fountain of living water" or are we just pacifying them, contenting ourselves with good morality and compliance? According to the book entitled "Get Rid of the Gimmicks," the author suggests that "we must admit that much of the youth ministry world has bought into the theory that the Bible alone cannot get the job done."

I somewhat agree with this statement about youth ministry. I'm guilty of thinking that we must use other tools besides the Bible as it relates to youth ministry. How many times have you tried to come up with a creative way to teach and ended up failing? If you are going to develop a Bible-based

youth ministry, you must first start with the Bible! We have to continue to preach the Bible to a generation that seems to be moving away from the Word of God. This helps them to learn the foundations of the Word before venturing out into the world at large. Ask yourself these questions:
- When did we begin to doubt the power of the Word?
- What happened to Hebrews 4:12?
- What kind of youth group is there for your sons and daughters right now?
- Are they learning and growing in truth?
- If your children are not being fed the truth, what hope can you have that they will be walking in the truth?

I know you are asking the question, how do I make the Bible fun and impactful for my youth group? In order for this to happen, you must follow these principles:

1. Spend time in God's Word daily.
2. Be intentional about learning their culture.
3. You must be able to bridge their culture and the Bible together.
4. Bring the Bible to life.
5. Consider interactive Bible Study sessions.

I challenge each of you as parents, youth pastors, and youth leaders to redefine your youth ministry. Establish the Word of God as a stronghold over your youth's life. Allow the Word of God to be a solid foundation for your youth ministry. I believe by taking this step and returning back to the basics, you will see a shift in your ministry as it relates to the maturity of your students.

# Chapter Six
## THE YOUTH PASTOR WITHIN

Throughout your tenure as youth leader of a particular ministry, plan to grow spiritually, intellectually, social emotionally, physically, and in your mission, and maintain that growth. Developing a "Rule of Life" in these areas will help you grow into what God has called you to be. "Rules of Life", is your personal holistic description of the Spirit-empowered rhythms and relationships that create, redeem, sustain and transform the life God invites you to humbly fulfill for the glory of Christ our Lord. Learning about the different "rules of life" has helped me take advantage of practices that I would not normally utilize. After much thought and prayer, I have decided to write my own "Rule of Life."

Your spiritual development is a very important aspect of your daily life. While a youth leader, plan to maintain your spiritual discipline by incorporating daily intercessory prayer. Make intercession for others and yourself a weekly practice in your life. Your goal should be to develop a daily intercessory prayer life that will require you to spend 5-10 minutes per day in prayer. Practicing this spiritual discipline will help you grow closer to God and develop your own spiritual retreat, helping you to have an inner peace for others and yourself. Your spiritual development is also important if you hope to be a senior pastor one day. Taking on these practices now will only help you when that time comes.

One more practice that I established in my spiritual journey is writing a daily devotional. Writing a daily devotional has inspired me to piece together my inner thoughts about my concerns and allow God to speak to me through writings. In the past, this has been very hard for me to do. I understood that this must be done in order to become a better person and a better spiritual role model. Many of the youth at my church look up to me spiritually. I believe that these practices will not only help me personally, but also help me to be prepared to teach a generation the importance of spiritual development. Growing up, the only spiritual growth I had was Sunday School and Bible Study. Now that I learned new spiritual development and practices, I can in return give to future generations that I serve in the present age.

Although my spiritual development is important, I believe that you must also be aggressive intellectually by creating proper study habits that will help you comprehend and relay messages according to what God has called you to do. I have always thought I had a deep understanding of Scripture until my first week in Dr. Slater's New Testament class. I knew then that I didn't know it all and I needed to spend more time reading and developing a new way to retain information. Being one year removed from my last college class, I knew I needed to spend more time developing good studying skills and a motivational plan so I could succeed in college. In developing a plan to help me gain knowledge and wisdom in the Word, I made it a point to study five hours on Monday, Friday and Sunday. This gave me 15 hours per week outside of class periods to study and develop a strong theological perspective of God.

My social life is a vital component to my success as a youth pastor, as well. It is my duty to maintain a well-balanced life inside and outside of ministry. After finding out my personality type from the Myers Briggs test, which helped me understand why I do what I do, I commit to spend time with my family every Friday and Saturday, taking my wife on a date twice a month, and taking my children to an activity they would like once a month. This helped me to practice living a well-balanced life.

It is also important to maintain your relationship with your friends and extended family. After learning that I am social by nature, I realized that I had recently neglected my extended family and friends. In an effort to make sure that this does not happen again, I make sure that I kept in contact with them by calling once week to check on them. Make sure that you balance your life with friends and loved ones.

Maintaining a physical well-being is another rule of life that you should implement. You have to understand with all the studying and fast-paced lifestyle, you can easily find yourself indulging in an unhealthy situation. It should be your goal to exercise two times a week by running at least 2 miles per week. If you go to a fast food restaurant, limit your portion size and inquire about salads and low calorie foods. This will help you to develop physical health and take control of your flesh.

Your complete wholeness is needed for the longevity of youth ministry. It very important that you take care of the youth leader within so that God can use you at your very best!

# No Compromise: An Urban Guide
## TO URBAN YOUTH MINISTRY
### VOLUME TWO

For many years, urban youth ministry has been limited to a specific ethnicity, geographical location, or low-income neighborhoods. African Americans have fit into the stigma of urban communities for many years. I believe urban youth ministry is not a specific group, but it has become a culture. Volume 2 of Urban Guide to Youth Ministry will be helpful material that will enhance your relationship with urban youth. We hope this guide helps you as a leader and ultimately brings young people to Christ. Here's what you will find in Volume 2:

- Outside-In Method
- Finding the Pulse of the Culture
- Entertained to Death
- Age Ain't Nothing but a Number
- Choosing Student Leaders
- How to Relate to Urban Youth
- Speaking to Urban Youth

## STAY CONNECTED

Thank you for purchasing No Compromise. Minister Bobby would like to stay connected with you! Here are a few ways that you can stay updated on new book releases, speaking engagements, youth ministry events, and more!

**WEBSITE** www.urbanyouthministry.com
**FACEBOOK** Bobby Hampton Jr.
**INSTAGRAM** Bobby Hampton Jr.
**PERISCOPE** Bobby Hampton Jr.
**EMAIL** bohampton83@gmail.com

www.ingramcontent.com/pod-product-compliance
Lightning Source LLC
Chambersburg PA
CBHW051711090426
42736CB00013B/2655